# Alphabets Are
# *Amazing* Animals

# Alphabets Are
## *Amazing* Animals

*Anushka Ravishankar*
*Christiane Pieper*

# Anteaters Adore

# Arithmetic

**B**aby

Buffaloes

*Blow*

Big Blue

Bubbles

# Careless

# Crocodiles

## Catch *Cold*

# Dull Donkeys Dance

Daily

**E**ight

Eels

Eat

Eleven

Eggs

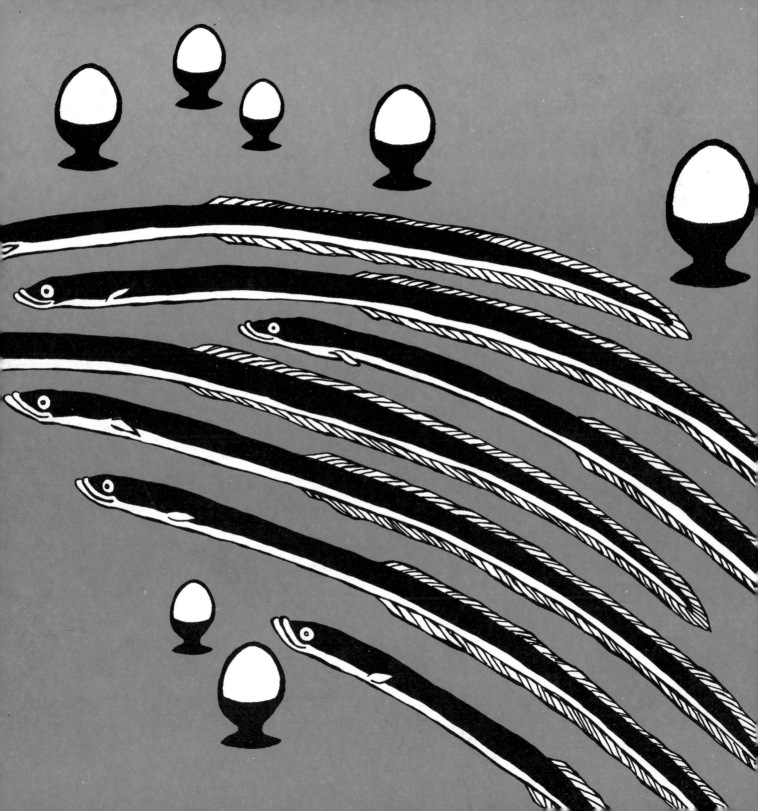

**F**at Fish

# Frighten

## Funny Frogs

**G**loomy Geese *Gobble* Grey Gum

Huge

# Hippos

## *Have*

### *Happy* Holidays

**I**ll

Iguanas

Imitate

Insects

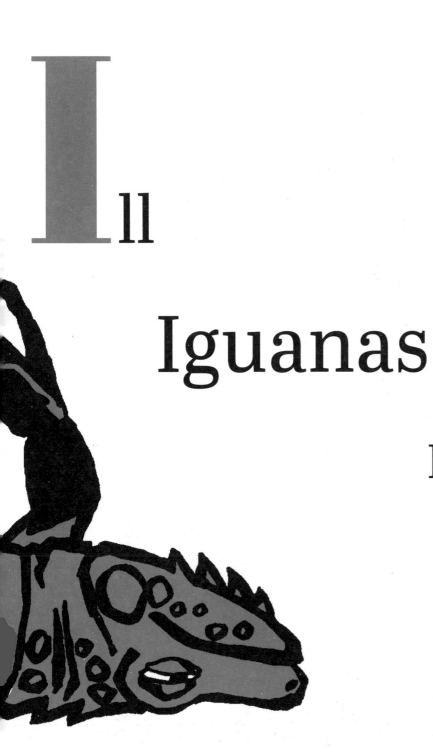

**J**olly

Jaguars

*Juggle*

Jam Jars

# Kind

Kiwis

*Kiss*

Kangaroos

**L**azy

Lions

*Lick*

Lollipops

# Messy Mice Make Macaroni

Neat Newts

Need

*Nappies*

# **O**dd

## Otters

### Order

*Only*

## Onions

**P***lump*

**Penguins**

*Play*

*Ping* *Pong*

**Q**uick

Quails

Queue

*Quietly*

**R**ude **R**abbits **R**ide **R**ed **R**oosters

**S**leepy Snails *Sing Silly* Songs

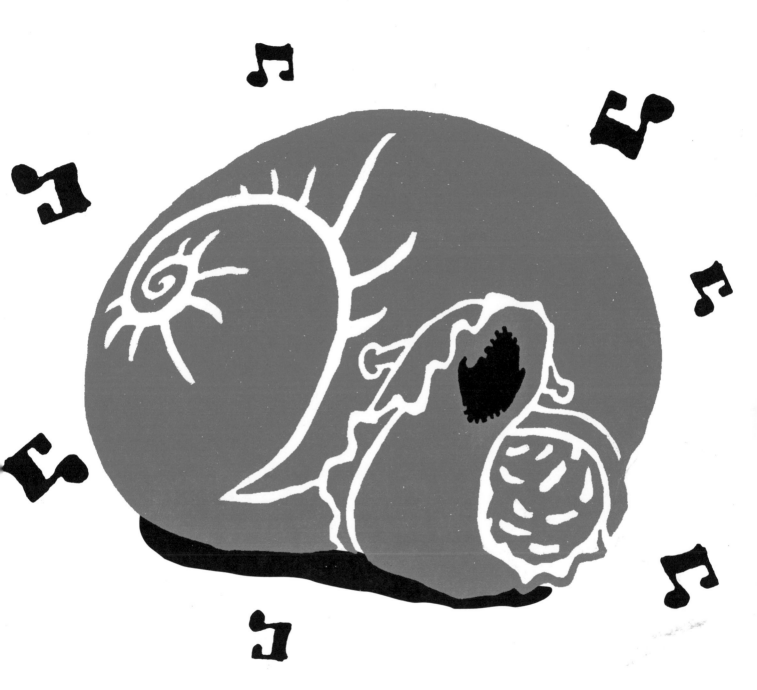

# Tiny Tadpoles

Tickle

Turtles

# Untidy

## Uakaris

### Use

### Upside-down

# *Umbrellas*

**V**ipers

*Visit*

Vultures

**W**et

Wolves

Walk

With

Weeping

Walruses

X emes

*X-ray*

Xemes

# Yaks

## YELL *Yahoooo*

# **Z**ebras

## Zoom

### *Zig-Zag*

Alphabets are *Amazing* Animals
Copyright © 2003 Tara Books Pvt. Ltd.
*For the text:* Anushka Ravishankar
*For the illustrations:* Christiane Pieper

Second edition 2015
For this edition:
Tara Books Pvt. Ltd., India
*www.tarabooks.com*
and
Tara Publishing Ltd., UK
*www.tarabooks.com/uk*

*Book design:* Rathna Ramanathan, Minus9 Design
*Production:* C. Arumugam

Printed in India by Sudarsan Graphics, Chennai

ISBN: 978-93-83145-25-6